The Poetry of Bliss Carman

Volume VIII - Last Songs From Vagabondia

Co-Authored with Richard Hovey

William Bliss Carman was born in Fredericton, in New Brunswick on April 15th 1861. He was educated at Fredericton Collegiate School before moving to the University of New Brunswick, obtaining his B.A. there in 1881. As is common with so many writers his first published piece was for the University magazine and for Carman that was in 1879.

After several years editing various magazines and periodicals Carman first published a poetry volume in 1893 with Low Tide on Grand Pré. There was no Canadian company prepared to publish and when an American company did so it went bankrupt.

The following year was decidedly better. His partnership with the American poet Richard Hovey had given birth to Songs of Vagabondia. It was an immediate success.

That success prompted the Boston firm, Stone & Kimball, to reissue Low Tide on Grand Pré and to hire Carman as the editor of its literary journal, The Chapbook.

Carman brought out, in 1895, Behind the Arras, a somewhat more serious and philosophical work centered on the premise of a long meditation, using the speaker's house and its many rooms, as a symbol of life and the choices to be made.

In 1896 Carman met Mrs Mary Perry King, who rapidly became patron, adviser and sometime lover. She also became his writing collaborator on two verse dramas.

In 1897 Carman published Ballad of Lost Haven, and in 1898, By the Aurelian Wall, the title poem itself was an elegy to John Keats and the book was a collection of formal elegies.

As the century turned Carman was hard at work on a five-volume set of poetry "Pans Pipes". The excellence of a number of these poems did much to install Carman as the most noted of Canadian Poets and eventually their own Poet Laureate.

In 1912 the final work in the Vagabondia series was published. Richard Hovey had died in 1900 and so this last work was purely Carman's. It has a distinct elegiac tone as if remembering the past works themselves.

On October 28th, 1921 Carman was honored by the newly-formed Canadian Authors' Association where he was crowned Canada's Poet Laureate with a wreath of maple leaves.

William Bliss Carman died of a brain hemorrhage at the age of 68 in New Canaan on the 8th June, 1929.

Index of Contents

AT THE CROSSROADS

You to the left and I to the right,
For the ways of men must sever —
And it well may be for a day and a night,
And it well may be forever.
But whether we meet or whether we part
(For our ways are past our knowing),
A pledge from the heart to its fellow heart
On the ways we all are going!
Here's luck!
For we know not where we are going.

We have striven fair in love and war,
But the wheel was always weighted;
We have lost the prize that we struggled for,
We have won the prize that was fated.
We have met our loss with a smile and a song,
And our gains with a wink and a whistle, —
For, whether we're right or whether we're wrong,
There's a rose for every thistle.
Here's luck —
And a drop to wet your whistle!

Whether we win or whether we lose
With the hands that life is dealing,
It is not we nor the ways we choose
But the fall of the cards that's sealing.
There's a fate in love and a fate in fight,
And the best of us all go under —
And whether we're wrong or whether we're right,
We win, sometimes, to our wonder.
Here's luck —
That we may not yet go under!

With a steady swing and an open brow
We have tramped the ways together,

But we're clasping hands at the crossroads now
In the Fiend's own night for weather;
And whether we bleed or whether we smile
In the leagues that lie before us,
The ways of life are many a mile
And the dark of Fate is o'er us.
Here's luck!
And a cheer for the dark before us!

You to the left and I to the right,
For the ways of men must sever,
And it well may be for a day and a night,
And it well may be forever!
But whether we live or whether we die
(For the end is past our knowing),
Here's two frank hearts and the open sky,
Be a fair or an ill wind blowing!
Here's luck!
In the teeth of all winds blowing.

"AT LAST, O DEATH"

A FRAGMENT

At last, O death!
Not with the sick-room fever and weary heart
And slow subsidence of diminished breath —
But strong and free
With the great tumult of the living sea.
Behold, I have loved.
And though I wept for the long sundering,
I did not fear thee, Death, nor then nor now.
I girded up my loins and sought my kind,
And did a man's work in a world of men,
And looked upon my work and called it good.
Now come, then, in the shape I love the best.
In the salt, sturdy wrestling of the sea,
I give thee welcome.

MAY AND JUNE

I

May comes, day comes,

One who was away comes;
All the earth is glad again,
Kind and fair to me.

May comes, day comes,
One who was away comes;
Set his place at hearth and board
As they used to be.

May comes, day comes,
One who was away comes;
Higher are the hills of home,
Bluer is the sea.

II

June comes, and the moon comes
Out of the curving sea,
Like a frail golden bubble,
To hang in the lilac tree.

June comes, and a croon comes
Up from the old gray sea,
But not the longed-for footstep
And the voice at the door for me.

PHILIP SAVAGE

Fields by Massachusetts Bay,
Where is he who yesterday

Called you Home, and loved to go
Where the cherry spreads her snow,

Through the purple misty woods
Of your soft spring solitudes,

Listening for the first fine gush
Of his fellow, the shy thrush —

Hearkening some diviner tone
Than our ears have ever known?

Woodland-musing by the hour
When the locust comes in flower,

He would watch by hill and swamp
Every sign of her green pomp

Where your matchless June once more
Leads her pageant up the shore.

Slopes of bayberry and fern,
While you wait for his return,

Can it be that he would test
Some far region of the West,

Tracking some great river course
To its undiscovered source?

Or an idler would he be
In the Islands of the Sea?

Can it be that he is gone,
Like so many a roving one,

The dread Arctic to explore,
Never to be heard of more —

Or with those who sail away
Every year from Gloucester Bay

For the Banks, and do not come
When the fishing fleets come home?

Stony uplands where the quail
Whistles by the pasture rail,

Where is one to whom you lent
Of your wise serene content,

Minstrel of your pagan psalm
With an Emersonian calm?

Open fields along the sea,
'T was your sweet sincerity

Made him what his fellows knew,
Sober, gentle, sane and true.

Whippoorwill and oriole,
He had your untarnished soul;

He your steadfast brother was,
Lowly field-bird of the grass.

Shores of Massachusetts Bay,
Teach us only in our day

Half as well your face to love
And your loving kindness prove.

Now the wind he loved so well
Makes the dune grass rock and swell,

And the marshy acres run
White with charlock in the sun,

Should he not be here to see
All your brave felicity!

Through these orchards green and dim,
Whose old calm was good to him,

Let the tiny yellow birds
Still repeat their shining words,

While across our senses steal
Hints of things no words reveal.

Let the air he used to know
From the iris meadows blow,

At evening through the open door
With the cool scents of the shore,

While across our spirits sweep
Sea-turns from a vaster deep.

Sunlit fields, how gently now
Your white daisies nod and bow,

Where the soft wind and the sun
Grieve not for a mortal one!

Only the old sea the more
Seems to whisper and deplore,

Murmuring like a childless crone
With her sorrow left alone —

The eternal human cry
To the heedless passer by.

Marshes, while your channels fill
And the June birds have their will,

While the elms along your edge
Wave above the rusty sedge,

And the bobolinks day long
Ply their juggleries of song,

While the sailing ships go by
To their ports below the sky,

Still the old Thalassian blue
Bounds this lovely world for you,

And the lost horizon lies
Past your wonder or surmise.

Fields by Massachusetts Bay,
When your questioner shall say,

"Where is he who should have been.
Poet of your lovely mien,

And your soul's interpreter?"
Answer, every larch and fir,

"He was here, but he is gone.
Some high purpose not his own

Summoned his unwasted powers
From our common woods and flowers.

All too soon from our abode
Back he wended to the road,

Rich in love, if not in fame.
Philip Savage was his name.

NON OMNIS MORIAR

IN MEMORY OF GLEESON WHITE

This paragraph cannot be true;
For such a man could not have died.
Death is so lonely, hard and cold, —
Not gentleness personified.

What manner was it in the man
That makes the story seem untrue?
Death is for fighters, rakes, and kings;
Malice nor greed he never knew.

He never seemed to strive to live;
His spirit was too sure for strife, —
Too glad, unquerulous and fair,
To take the sordid tinge of life.

The pompous folly of the world
Could never touch that radiant mien;
He moved unstained among the crowd,
Loyal, courageous, and serene.

No bargainer for wealth nor fame
Nor place, his was a better part, —
The simple love of all his kind,
And lifelong fervour in his art.

It must have been his charity,
That tender human heart of his,
That rare unfailing kindliness,
Could make his death seem so amiss.

In London where he lived and toiled,
I saw him smile across the throng,
The unembittered smile of those
Whose sweetness triumphs over wrong.

With that unvexed Chaucerian mood,
That zest unsevered from repose,
He is as wise as Omar now,
Or any Master of the Rose.

And here in the November dusk
There comes an echo, faint and far,
Of that gay, valiant, careless voice
That cried, Non omnis moriar!

Behind the mask of lore and creed
There dwells an instinct, strong and blind,

Refuting sorrow, bidding grief
Be something better than resigned.

There is a part of me that knows,
Beneath incertitude and fear,
I shall not perish when I pass
Beyond mortality's frontier;

But greatly having joyed and grieved,
Greatly content, shall hear the sigh
Of the strange wind across the lone
Bright lands of taciturnity.

In patience therefore I await
My friend's unchanged benign regard,—
Some April when I too shall be
Spilt water from a broken shard.

DAY AND NIGHT

(Read at the Sixty-sixth Annual Convention of the Psi Upsilon Fraternity, at Cornell University, 1899.)

Fair college of the quiet inland lake
And beautiful fair name that like a bell
Rings out its clear sheer call of joy, Cornell! —
Its call of high undaunted dares that take
The hearts of men with fervours for thy sake
And for thy sake with sudden hopes that swell,
Hail first to thee, with praise for thy bold youth,
Thy fearless challenge in the ranks of truth,
Thy forward footing into the unknown!
The new in knowledge that is old in being
Wrenched from the dark and morninged for our seeing —
This is the legend on thy banners blown.

Mightier the foes yet that are still to smite,
And fiercer yet the fields we still must fight,
But thou, a David of the sunrise cause,
In the first dawn of the defiant day,
Startled the mumbling hosts that bar the way —
Thou, a young Spartan of the days to be,
Made the vast hordes of Persian darkness pause
And bade our band think of Thermopylae.

Day — yes, the day for thee! but all we men
Are twofold, having need of day and night.

Day for the mind, the ardour of the fight,
Night for the soul and silence. So again
To thee I turn, O one of many stars
That make the loyal heaven glorious
But dear among the innumerable to us,
Psi Upsilon, and resting from the scars
Of day, the brunt of battle, lift thy song,
"Now for the joys of night! " — they sing it still
In the old chapters where we had our fill
Of fun and fellowship and frank good will,
I and my fellows, when we too were young.
"Soft as a dream of beauty" — hark, again!
Here's to his right good health who sang that strain!

Come with me into the night —
The intimate embracing night!
The night is still;
And we may walk from hill to hill
Silent, with but the murmur of our souls,
As through the woods the murmur of the night.
— Ah, take your heaven of undying light,
Of glare of gold and glint of aureoles!
I think God keeps for us somewhere
A place of cool dusks and caressing air,
Where all the greens and yellows dream of blue
And all the rainbow hints itself in hue
But never speaks outright, —
Never unveils
The unmistakable red or violet,
But lets all colour die to a perfume.

Is it the flapping of sails
And the lurch of a jibing boom
Where a boat comes round, below, on the lake, to set
Off shore again? How clear,
Like the league-distant hills that seem so near
In the thin air of Colorado, rise
The voices of the merry-making crew
Over the waters, — songs of love that strew
The silence with the roses of surmise!

Hark!

There is no sound beneath the sky
But sails that flap and oars that feather
And the low water whispering by
In the June weather,
My love and I,

My love and I,
My love and I together!

The starlight lies upon the lake
Like dreams of vanished days and viewless
Earth never shall recall awake, —
The dim lost Thules!
My love and I,
My love and I,
My love and I together!

The soft wind stirs among the firs,
The great stars wait above and seek not;
The night is full of ministers
For souls that speak not.
My love and I,
My love and I,
My love and I together!

I wonder whether you and I
Are real, love — I wonder whether!
I only know that, live or die,
We dream together.
My love and I,
My love and I,
My love and I together!

Far, so far —
The song dies on the waters like a star
That founders in the surges of the dawn.

Ah, the great Night!
The far phantasmal Night!
The delicate dim aisles and domes of dream!
Loosed from the mind, set free
From thought and memory,
The soul goes naked into the vast stream
Of musing spirit like a careless Faun, —
The soul lies naked to the summer night.

Night of the clasped hands of comrades! Night of the kiss
Of lovers trembling at love's mysteries!
Night of desire!
Night of the gaslight-necklaced city! Night
Of revel and laughter and delight!
Night of the starlit Sea!
Night of the waves shot with strange witch-fire!
Night of sleep!

Night of dream!
Night of the lonely soul under the stars!

But ever the self put away
With the day,
And the soul soaring, glorying into the night!

Night!
The masked mysterious Night!
The infinite unriddled beautiful Witch!
The Sibyl of the universal Doom!

This is the joy of man's spirit —
When peace falls,
Unknown, undivined, inexplicable,
Over the face of the world.

Oh, praise for the glory of battle — the Day and its strife!
And praise for the sweat and the struggle, the turmoil of life!
But the work is not wrought for the working, increase for increase;
We toil for the rest that comes after, we battle for peace.

Let us take up our work every man, meet our fate with a cheer —
But the best is the clasped hands of comrades, when nightfall is near,
The best is the rest and the friendship, the calm of the soul
When the stars are in heaven and the runner lies down at the goal.
Let us take up our work as a nation, the work of the day,
Clasp hands with our brothers of England — and who shall say nay?
And who shall say nay to our navies — the ships of us, sons of the Sea?
And who shall say nay to our Empires, to the Law that we set for the free?
But the best is the bond that's between us, the bond of the brothers in blood,
The bond of the men who keep silence, as the night when it falls on the flood,
As the night when it falls on the vastness, the splendour and lone of the wave,
The bond of the English forever, the bond of the free and the brave!

And at last when the bugles are silent or call but to rouse
A cheer for the memory of crowned and victorious brows,
When the drums beat no more to the battle and, smitten in one,
The hearts of the nations uplift but one song to the sun,
When, the Law once made good for all peoples by stress of the sword,
The spent world shall rest from its wrestling, clasp hands in accord,
Then, best of all bests, in the silence that falls on man's soul,
We shall feel we are comrades and brothers from tropic to pole.
All men by the pledge of their manhood made one in the will
To achieve for all men as their fellows each conquest o'er ill,
No glory or beauty or music or triumph or mirth
If it be not made good for the least of the sons of the earth,
And the bond of all bonds shall be manhood, the right of all rights

The right to the hearts of our fellows, to the love that requites
All the strain and the pain and the fag, all the wrench of the day,
When the stars shine at last in the heavens and Night has its way.

THE BATTLE OF MANILA

A FRAGMENT

By Cavite on the bay
'T was the Spanish squadron lay;
And the red dawn was creeping
O'er the city that lay sleeping
To the east, like a bride, in the May.
There was peace at Manila,
In the May morn at Manila, —

When ho, the Spanish admiral
Awoke to find our line
Had passed by gray Corregidor,
Had laughed at shoal and mine,
And flung to the sky its banners
With "Remember" for a sign!

With the ships of Spain before
In the shelter of the shore,
And the forts on the right,
They drew forward to the fight,
And the first was the gallant Commodore;
In the bay of Manila,
In the doomed bay of Manila —
With succour half the world away,
No port beneath that sky,
With nothing but their ships and guns
And Yankee pluck to try,
They had left retreat behind them,
They had come to win or die!

For we spoke at Manila,
We said it at Manila,
Oh be ye brave, or be ye strong,
Ye build your ships in vain;
The children of the sea queen's brood
Will not give up the main;
We hold the sea against the world
As we held it against Spain.

Be warned by Manila,
Take warning by Manila,
Ye may trade by land, ye may fight by land.
Ye may hold the land in free;

But go not down to the sea in ships
To battle with the free;
For England and America
Will keep and hold the sea!

THE CITY IN THE SEA

Once of old there stood a fabled city
By the Breton sea,
Towered and belled and flagged and wreathed and pennoned
For the pomp of Yuletide revelry;
All its folk, adventurous, sea-daring,
Gay as gay could be.

And at night when window, torch, and bonfire
Lighted up the sky,
Down the wind came galleon and pinnace,
Steered for that red lantern, riding high;
Every brown hand hard upon the tiller,
Shoreward every eye.

Well I see that hardy Breton sailor
With the bearded lip, —
How he laughed out, holding his black racer
Where the travelling sea-hills climb and slip,
Chased by storm and lighted on to haven,
Ship by homing ship.

Every sail came in, like deep-sea rovers
Who have heard afar
Wild and splendid hyperborean rumours
Of a respite made to feud and war, —
Making port where sea-wreck and disaster
Should not vex them more.

What of Ys? Where was it when gray morning
Gloomed o'er Brittany?
Smothered out in elemental fury,
Wrecked and whelmed in the engulfing sea,
To become the name of a sea-story
In lost legendry.

In my heart there is a sunken city,
Wonderful as Ys.
All day long I hear the mellow tolling
Of its sweet-sad lonely bells of peace,
Rocked by tides that wash through all its portals
Without let or cease.

Pale and fitful as the wan auroras
Are its nights and days;
In from nowhere flush the drafty sea-turns
By forgotten and neglected ways;
Through the entries and the doors of being
That faint music strays;

Tolling back the wandered and the way-worn
From far alien lands;
Tolling back the gipsy child of beauty
With mysterious and soft commands;
Tolling back the spirit that within me
Hears and understands.

Then some May night, with a scent of lilacs
In the magic air,
Through the moonlight and the mad spring weather,
(Old love's fervour and new love's despair),
I go down to my familiar city,
Roaming court and square.

Of a sudden at a well-known corner,
In the densest throng,
Unexpected at the very moment
As an April robin's gush of song,
Some one smiles; and there's the perfect comrade
I have missed so long.

Then, at just the touch of hand on shoulder
Bidding grief be gone,
I forget the loneliness of travel
For the while the parted ways are one, —
Know the meaning of the world's great gladness
Underneath the sun.

That's the story of my sounding sea-bells,
Chiming all night long, —
The eternal cadence of sea-sorrow
For Man's lot and immemorial wrong, —
The lost strain that haunts this human dwelling

With a ghost of song.

Nay, but is there any lost sea-city
Buried in the main,
Where we shall go down in days hereafter,
Having said good-bye to grief and pain,
Joy and love at last made one with beauty,
Glad and free again?

You believe not? Hark, there comes the tolling
Of my bells once more,
That far-heard and faint fantastic music
From my city by the perilous shore,
Sounding the imperious allegiance
I shall not deplore.

THE LANTERNS OF ST. EULALIE

In the October afternoon
Orange and purple and maroon,

Goes quiet Autumn, lamp in hand,
About the apple-coloured land,

To light in every apple-tree
The Lanterns of St. Eulalie.

They glimmer in the orchard shade
Like fiery opals set in jade, —

Crimson and russet and raw gold,
Yellow and green and scarlet old.

And O when I am far away
By foaming reel or azure bay,

In crowded street or hot lagoon,
Or under the strange austral moon, —

When the homesickness comes on me
For the great Marshes by the sea,

The running dikes, the brimming tide,
And the dark firs on Fundy side,

In dream once more I shall behold,

Like signal lights, those globes of gold

Hung out in every apple-tree —
The Lanterns of St. Eulalie.

HOLIDAY

What is this joy to-day,
Hope, reparation, reprieve?

Out of the sweltering city,
Out of the blaring streets
And narrow houses of men,
The seaboard express for the North
Forges, and settles for flight
Into the great blue summer,
The wide, sweet, opulent noon.

Farewell despondency, fear,
Ambition, and pitiless greed,
And sordid unlovely regrets!
And thou, frail spirit in me,
My journey-fellow these years,
Behold, thy brothers the elms,
And thy sisters the daisies, are here.
Thou, too, shalt grow and be glad,
Companioned of innocence now,
In the long hours of joy.

How will it be that day,
When the dark train is ready,
And the inexorable gong
Sounds on the platform of Time

MARIGOLDS

The marigolds are nodding;
I wonder what they know.
Go, listen very gently;
You may persuade them so.

Go, be their little brother,
As humble as the grass,
And lean upon the hill-wind,

And watch the shadows pass.

Put off the pride of knowledge,
Put by the fear of pain;
You may be counted worthy
To live with them again.

Be Darwin in your patience,
Be Chaucer in your love;
They may relent and tell you
What they are thinking of.

A PRELUDE

This is the sound of the Word
From the waters of sleep,
The rain-soft voice that was heard
On the face of the deep,
When the fog was drawn back like a veil, and the sentinel tides
Were given their thresholds to keep.

The South Wind said, "Come forth,"
And the West Wind said, "Go far!"
And the silvery sea-folk heard,
Where their weed tents are,
From the long slow lift of the blue through the Carib keys,
To the thresh on Sable bar.

This is the Word that went by,
Over sun-land and swale,
The long Aprilian cry,
Clear, joyous, and hale,
When the summons went forth to the wild shy broods of the air,
To bid them once more to the trail.

The South Wind said, "Come forth,"
And the West Wind said, "Be swift!"
And the fluttering sky-folk heard,
And the warm dark thrift
Of the nomad blood revived, and they gathered for flight,
By column and pair and drift.

This is the sound of the Word
From bud-sheath and blade,
When the reeds and the grasses conferred,
And a gold beam was laid

At the taciturn doors of the forest, where tarried the Sun,
For a sign they should not be dismayed.

The South Wind said, "Come forth,"
And the West Wind said, "Be glad!"
The abiding wood-folk heard,
In their new green clad,
Sanguine, mist-silver, and rose, while the sap in their veins
Welled up as of old all unsad.

This is the Word that flew
Over snow-marsh and glen,
When the frost-bound slumberers knew,
In tree-trunk and den,
Their bidding had come, they questioned not whence nor why, —
They reckoned not whither nor when.

The South Wind said, "Come forth,"
And the West Wind said, "Be wise!"
The wintering ground-folk heard,
Put the dark from their eyes,
Put the sloth from sinew and thew, to wander and dare, —
Forever the old surmise!

This is the Word that came
To the spirit of Man,
And shook his soul like a flame
In the breath of a fan,
Till it burned as a light in his eyes, as a colour that grew
And prospered under the tan.

The South Wind said, "Come forth,"
And the West Wind said, " Be free! "
Then he rose and put on the new garb,
And knew he should be
The master of knowledge and joy, though sprung from the tribes
Of the earth and the air and the sea.

THE NORTHERN MUSE

The Northern Muse looked up
Into the ancient tree,
Where hang the seven olives,
And twine the roses three.

I heard, like the eternal
Susurrus of the sea,

Her Scire quod sciendum
Da mihi, Domine!

THE TIME AND THE PLACE

"Never the time and the place
And the loved one all together!"
Ah, Browning, that does to tell!
But I have an eagle feather
Hid in my waistcoat too.

Yes, once in the wild June weather,
In God's own North befell
The joy not time shall undo
Nor the storm of years efface.
Ah, master Browning, you hear?

If ever the time and the place
With aught of thy mood concur,
Far off in my golden year,
The solstice of my prime,
Youth done, age not begun,
The moment that soul is ripe
For the little touch of rhyme,
Then hearken! If there but stir
One breath of the Spirit of earth
Through me his frail reed-pipe,
(As the hermit-thrush
Rehearses the scene when the joy of the world had birth,
So sure, so fine,
Disturbing the hush,)
You shall hearken, and hear
Take rapture and sense and form in one perfect line
A golden lyric of Her!

UNDER THE ROWANS

I saw a little river
Running beside a wall,
And over it hung scarlet
The berried rowans tall.

Beside it for a moment
The summer-time delayed;

And cooler fell the sunlight
Through centuries of shade.

And there was laughing Bronwen
A-wading to the knee.
While still the foolish water
Went racing to the sea.

I whistled, "Love, come over!"
She was too wild to fear
The wildness of the forest,
The ruin of the year.

And when the stars above us
Hung in the rowans high,
It was the little river
That made our lullaby.

Indoors, to-night, and fire-dreams!
And where I wander, far
Within a shining country
That needs no calendar,

There is a little river
Running beside a wall,
And over it hang scarlet
The berried rowans tall.

THE GIRL IN THE POSTER

FOR A DESIGN BY ETHEL REED

With her head in the golden lilies,
She reads and is never done.
Why her girlish face so still is,
I know not under the sun.

She is the soul of a woman,
Knowing whatever befalls;
And I a lonely human,
Dwelling within her walls.

She is the fair immortal
Daughter of truth and art;
And I, at her lowly portal,
May fare and be glad and depart,

In a region forever vernal,
She keeps her lilied state, —
My beautiful calm eternal
Mysteriarch of fate.

In a volume great and golden,
Would better beseem a sage,
Her downcast look is holden;
But I cannot see the page.

Picture, or printed column,
Or records, or cipherings, —
From the drooping lids so solemn
I guess at marvellous things.

Is it a rune she ponders, —
Word from an outer clime,
Where the spirit quests and wanders
Through long sidereal time?

Would she trammel her heart, or cumber
Her mind with our mortal needs?
Do the shadows quake and slumber
On the book wherein she reads?

I know not. I know her being
Is impulse and mood to mine,
Till I voyage, without foreseeing
For a lost horizon line.

For her the spacious morrow;
But the humble day for me,
In the little house of sorrow
By the unbefriending sea.

Her hair is a raven glory;
Her chin is pointed and small;
What is the wonderful story
Keeps her forever in thrall?

Her mouth is little and childly;
Her brow is innocent broad;
Meekly she reads and mildly, —
Would neither condemn nor applaud.

Would that I too, a-reading,
Might half of her wisdom find,

In the gold flowers there unheeding, —
The calm of an open mind!

Day long, as I keep the homely
Round of my chambers here,
Her beauty is modest and comely,
Her presence living and near.

Till it seems I must recover
A day in the ilex grove,
Where I was a destined lover,
And she was destined for love.

I remember the woods we strayed in,
And the mountain paths we trod,
When she was a Doric maiden,
And I was a young Greek god.

And I have the haunting fancy,
The moment my back is turned,
By some Eastern necromancy
Only the artists have learned,

Two great grave eyes are lifted
To follow me round the room,
And a sudden breath has shifted
A leaf in the Book of Doom.

ON THE STAIRS

From glory up to glory
On the great stairs of time,
I track the ghostly whisper
That bids a mortal climb.

I pass the gorgeous threshold
Of many an open door,
Where, luring and illusive,
The pageant gleams once more.

Up the Potomac Valley
I see the April come;
Here it is May in Paris;
Here is my Ardise home;

These are the Scituate marshes;

This is a Norman town;
These are the dikes of Grand Pré; —
Ah, tell no more, Renown!

I pass the open portals,
Irresolute and fond, —
Desert the masque of beauty
For Beauty's self beyond.

For down the echoing stairway
Of being, I have heard
The faint immortal secret
Shut in a mortal word, —

The tawny velvet accent
Of Lilith, as she came
Into the great blue garden
And breathed her lover's name.

THE DESERTED INN

I came to a deserted inn,
Standing apart, alone;
A place where human joy had been,
And only winds made moan.

I entered by the spacious hall,
With not a soul to see;
The echo of my own footfall
Was ghostly there to me.

I came upon a sudden door,
Which gave me no reply;
The more I questioned it, the more
A questioner was I.

I lingered by the mouldy stair,
And by the dusty sill;
And when my faint heart said, "Beware!"
The silence said, "Be still!"

From room to room I caught the stir
Of garments vanishing, —
The stillness trying to demur,
When one has ceased to sing.

Like shadows of the clouds which make
The loneliness of noon,
The thing I could not overtake
Was but an instant gone.

'T was summer when I reached the inn;
The apples were in bloom;
Before I left, the snow drove in,
The frost was like a doom.

At last I came upon the book
Where visitors of yore
Had writ their names, ere joy forsook
The House of Rest-no-more.

Poor fellow-travellers, beset
With hungers not of earth!
Did you, too, tarry here in debt
For things of perished worth?

Did something lure you like a strain
Of music wild and vast,
Only to freeze your blood again
With jeers when you had passed?

Did visions of a fairer thing
Than God has ever made
Fleet through your doorways in the spring,
And would not be delayed?

Did beauty in a half-made song,
A smile of mystery,
Departing, leave you here to long
For what could never be, —

And thenceforth you were friends of peace,
Acquainted with unrest,
Whom no perfection could release
From the unworldly quest?

I heard a sound of women's tears,
More desolate than the sea,
Sigh through the chambers of the years
Unto eternity.

And then beyond the fathom of sense
I knew, as the dead know,
My lost ideal had journeyed thence

Unnumbered years ago.

And from that dwelling of the night,
With the gray dusk astir,
I waited for the first gold light
To let me forth to Her.

THE OPEN DOOR

Love me, love me not, —
What is that to me?
I have not forgot
When we two were three.

She who loved us twain
Well enough to die, —
Can we love again
While her ghost stands by?

Love me, love me not, —
I can love no more,
For the empty cot
And the open door.

JAPANESE LOVE-SONG

How you start away!
— As a flame starts from a gust.
Flame-heart o' the dust!
Sudden startle of dismay!
Swift triumph in distrust!

Flash and tremble of escape,
Fierce with desire!
Rippled water shot with fire
Wary of the rape
Of the eyes that sire!

Radiant no-and-yes!
Deer-flight and panther-thirst!
Blest and accurst!
Sword-splendour past the guess
Of Heaven's best and Hell's worst!

So you sprang up from yourself,
Burnt to supremacies,
Star-demoned by a kiss —
Night turned fire-elf, —
Wonder and all amiss!

"HOW SHOULD LOVE KNOW?"

How should Love know
The face of sorrow?
Love is so young a thing!
Roses that blow
To-day, lie to-morrow
Faded and withering.

UNFORESEEN

Why did I kiss you, sweet?
Nor you nor I can say.
You might have said some commonplace,
I might have turned away.

No thought was in our hearts
Of what we were to be.
Fate sent a madness on our souls
And swept us out to sea.

Fate, between breath and breath,
Has made the world anew,
And the bare skies of yesterday
Are all aflame with you.

CHILD'S SONG

But just across the furthest hill
I know the fairies live.

Please, sir, take me in your carriage
And ride me home! You see,
I've been to find the fairies
And I'm tired as I can be.

I crossed the meadow and the brook
And climbed Rapalye's hill,
But when I reached the top of it
There was another still.

HARMONICS

"Truth is not a creed,
For it does not need
Ever an apology.
Truth is not an ology;
'T is not part, but all.
Priests and savans shall
Never solve the mystic
Problem. The artistic
Mind alone of all can tell
What is Truth.

"Poet, thou art wisest;
Dogmas thou despisest —
Science little prizest.
Tell us, for thou knowest well,
What is Truth."

Spake the seekers to an holy
Bard, who answered, mild and lowly —
This, all this, was in the olden
Days when Saturn's reign was golden —

"Shall I read the riddle —
Tell you what is Truth?
Truth is not the first
Not the last or middle;
'T is the beautiful
And symmetric whole,
Embracing best and worst,
Embracing age and youth.

"All the universe
Is one mighty song,
Wherein every star
Chants out loud and strong
Each set note and word
It must aye rehearse.
Though the parts may jar,
The whole is as one chord."

ORNITHOLOGY

Sweetheart, do you see up yonder
through the leaves
The elm tree interweaves,
How that cock-sparrow chases his brown mate?
Look, where she perches now
Upon the bough
And turns her head to see if he pursue her,
Half frightened, half elate
To have so bold and beautiful a wooer.
See, he alights beside her. How his wings
Quiver with amorous passionings!
How voluble their chattering courtship is!
Soon will he know
Love's joys in overflow,
Love's extreme ecstasies.

No, off she flies!
Just as she seemed about to be subdued
To his impetuous desire!
How angrily he scolds, with wicked eyes
Following her flight, and turns his tiny ire
Against the innocent tree and pecks the wood!
While she — ah, the coquette —!
Lurks yonder in the cleft where the great tree
Breaks into boughs, and peeps about to see
If he is coming yet.
She's in for a game of lovers' hide-and-seek,
And longs to have him find the hiding-place,
Although she feigns concealment, so to pique
His passion to a chase.

In vain — he will not look
For all her sweet allurements. Out she whisks
Demurely from her nook,
As if she did not see and were not seen,
And perks herself and frisks
Her delicate tail as a lady flirts her fan,
And now slips back again to her retreat
And waits for one hushed moment in serene
Unfluttered expectation that the plan
Have issue sweet.
What, will he not come yet?
See how she glances at him unawares,

Tosses her head and gives herself high airs
In such a pretty pet.

Cruel! he turns away,
Affecting unconcern.
All those endearing wiles are wrought in vain.
Alas, unlucky flirt! too late you learn
That long delays will make the eagerest lover
Aweary of pursuing. Nay,
Too late you fly half way to him again.
You will not so recover.
The passion that you played with. Off he flies
And now is lost in the thick shade
Of lilac bushes further down the glade.
Another mistress charms his amorous eyes.
Have a care, sweetheart, or as he some day
I too will fly away.

TO AN IRIS

Thou art a golden iris
Under a purple wall,
Whereon the burning sunlight
And greening shadows fall.

What Summer night's enchantment
Took up the garden mould,
And with the falling star-dust
Refined it to such gold?

What wonder of white magic
Bidding thy soul aspire,
Filled that luxurious body
With languor and with fire?

Wert thou not once a beauty
In Persia or Japan,
For whom, by toiling seaway
Or dusty caravan,

Of old some lordly lover
Brought countless treasure home
Of gems and silk and attar,
To pleasure thee therefrom?

Pale amber from the Baltic,

Soft rugs of Indian ply,
Stuffs from the looms of Bagdad
Stained with the Tyrian dye.

Were thy hands bright with henna,
Thy lashes black with kohl,
Thy voice like silver water
Out of an earthen bowl?

Or was thy only tent-cloth
The blue Astartean night,
Thy soul to beauty given,
Thy body to delight?

Wert thou not well desired,
And was not life a boon,
When Tanis held in Sidon
Her Mysteries of the Moon?

There in her groves of ilex
The nightingales made ring
With the mad lyric chorus
Of youth and love and Spring,

Wert thou not glad to worship
With some blond Paphian boy,
Illumined by new knowledge
And intimate with joy?

And did not the Allmother
Smile in the hushed dim light,
Hearing thy stifled laughter
Disturb her holy rite?

Ah, well thou must have served her
In wise and gracious ways,
With more than vestal fervour,
A loved one all thy days!

And dost thou, then, revisit
Our borders at her will,
Child of the sultry rapture,
Waif of the Orient still?

Because thy love was fearless
And fond and strong and free,
Art thou not her last witness
To our apostasy?

Just at the height of summer,
The joy-days of the year,
She bids, for our reproval,
Thy radiance appear.

Oh, Iris, let thy spirit
Enkindle our gross clay,
Bring back the lost earth-passion
For beauty to our day!

To-night, when down the marshes
The lilac half-lights fade,
And on the rosy shore-line
No earthly spell is laid,

I would be thy new lover,
With the dark life renewed
By our great mother Tanis
And thy solicitude.

Feel slowly change this vesture
Of mortal flesh and bone,
Transformed by her soft witch-work
To one more like thine own.

Become but as the rain-wind
(Who am but dust indeed),
To slake thy velvet ardour
And soothe thy darling need.

To dream and waken with thee
Under the night's blue sail,
As the wild odours freshen,
Till the white stars grow pale.

BERRIS YARE

A LEGEND OF THE BRIER ROSE

Once in the fairy tale sweet Rose Brier
Climbed to the bent of her heart's desire.
Poor Rose Brier, as I've heard tell,
Never came back with her folk to dwell.

This is the legend of sweet Brier Rose

Out of a country that nobody knows.
Dear Brier Rose could never aspire,
Yet came at length to her heart's desire.

Single-Heart Brier Rose, gipsy desire
Eyes of the Hush-hound and crispy dark hair,
Lyric of summer dawn, dew-drench and fire,
Wilding and gentle and shy Berris Yare!

Bide with me, Brier Rose, here for an hour.
See the red sun, like a great royal rose,
Flung down the gray for the winter's king flower,
While Marden sleeps in his mantle of snows.

Far-wandered Brier Rose, how came we here,
Alien, ease-loving, alone in this North?
White winter, laid at the heart of the year,
Heeds us not, needs us not, leads us not forth.

Long ago, Brier Rose, loved we not thus?
Was it when Alaric marched against Rome?
Others might win the world: leave love for us!
Dost thou remember the Visigoth home?

Think again, Summer-heart. Canst not recall
When thou wert Brier Rose gladsome and fair?
How I remember thee, shapely and tall, —
Far away, long ago thee, Berris Yare!

Sword-play for Brier Rose, war song and march;
Throstle for joy bade the waking world sing;
Morning waved banners out bold from the larch;
When we went down on the legions in spring.

Bracelets for Brier Rose, wrought Roman gold;
Tribute and trophy poured plenty as sand;
Frost on the flower-garth, rime on the wold;
When we came triumphing back through the land.

How thy cheek, Brier Rose, signalled aflame;
How the song rang of the foemen downborne;
How the brown eyes kindled up as we came
Through the bowed ranks of the gleaming red corn!

Then the long days when the harvest was done;
Hand in hand, hill and dale, thou and I there,
Dreaming of far-off new isles of the sun, —
Never a dream of this day, Berris Yare!

Fairy-tale, home-royal red of the rose,
Wilding and well-a-day sweet of the brier!
Here in the gray world engirdled with snows,
Watch the slow sun set the hilltops afire!

What if, my Brier Rose, love were just this:
One gracious core of the whirled starry dust,
Round which the swinging motes, never amiss,
Traverse the infinite dark as they must.

All the earth else a mere seed-plot of clay,
Fruitless and flowerless, mixed garden mould,
Awaiting the gardener, inert, to obey
When the first sunbeam bids, "Blossoms, unfold!"

Then the whole host of them, gold daffodils;
Poppies so well of red dreamland aware;
Michaelmas daisies smoke blue on the hills;
None like my Brier Rose, my Berris Yare.

Acres of apple-bloom, maids at the door;
Wind-hands of summer with heart-strings to pull;
Fruit to the harvesting, men to the war;
Come winter speedily, love's year is full.

Cherry-mouth Brier Rose, washed in the dew,
Kiss me again before daylight be done, —
Once for the old love and twice for the new,
Thrice for the dearest love under the sun!

Gold heart of sundowns and summers forgot!
Treasure of solitude, simple and wild!
God in our poem missed rhyme by a jot;
Life never yet with poor love reconciled.

Wert thou not Brier Rose once on a time?
Attar of memory, chivalry's dare!
Love's the lost echo of flute-notes at prime,
Wondrous, far wandering. Hark, Berris Yare!

Only the leaves of the oaks brown and sere,
Garrulous wiseacre, doting old leaves,
Go whisper others your cumber-world fear, —
Kill-joy foreboding that croaks and deceives!

Heed them not, Brier Rose. Hearken again!
Nothing? No breath of the music to be?

Ah! but I hear the low footfall of rain, —
April's clan Joy making in from the sea.

April. Think, Brier Rose! how the earth's heart,
Brook rapture, bird rapture, riot of rills,
Stirs with old dreams that rend slumber apart!
Then the long twilight dim-blue on the hills.

Hills that will talk to me when thou art gone, —
That old solicitude, calming despair,
Sweet as the sundown, austere as the dawn, —
"Love that lost Brier Rose, found Berris Yare."

April. Then, Brier Rose, some silent eve,
While the dusk hears the hill-rivers give tongue,
In the first swamp-robin I shall perceive
One golden strain that, when being was young,

Kin to the world-cry and kith to the stars,
Pierced human sorrows such ages ago.
Leisurely fluting in gold, broken bars
Comes the rehearsal, serenely and slow,

Prelude, re-prelude; and then the full throat,
Mellowly, mellowly — stops mid-stream —
Wearily, wearily. — What may denote
Such incompleteness? Can love be the theme?

Brother of Brier Rose, flute-master mine
(Then will this heart-ache out cry to him there),
Thou with the secret in that flute of thine,
Where is my dream-fellow, lost Berris Yare?

A MODERN ECLOGUE

SHE
If you were ferryman at Charon's ford,
And I came down the bank and called to you,
Waved you my hand and asked to come aboard,
And threw you kisses there, what would you do?

Would there be such a crowd of other girls,
Pleading and pale and lonely as the sea,
You'd growl in your old beard, and shake your curls,
And say there was no room for little me?

Would you remember each of them in turn?
Put all your faded fancies in the bow,
And all the rest before you in the stern,
And row them out with panic on your brow?

If I came down and offered you my fare
And more beside, could you refuse me there?

HE

If I were ferryman in Charon's place,
And ran that crazy scow with perilous skill,
I should be so worn out with keeping trace
Of gibbering ghosts and bidding them sit still,

If you should come with daisies in your hands,
Strewing their petals on the sombre stream, —
"He will come," and "He won't come," down the lands
Of pallid reverie and ghostly dream, —

I would let every clamouring shape stand there,
And give its shadowy lungs free vent in vain,
While you with earthly roses in your hair,
And I grown young at sight of you again,

Went down the stream once more at half-past seven
To find some brand-new continent of heaven.

FROM THE CLIFF

Here on this ledge, the broad plain stretched below,
The calm hills smiling in immortal mirth,
The blue sky whitening as it nears the earth,
Afar where all the summits are aglow,
I feel a mighty wind upon me blow
Like God's breath kindling in my soul a birth
Of turbulent music struggling to break girth.
I pass with Dante through eternal woe,
Quiver with Sappho's passion at my heart,
See Pindar's chariots flashing past the goal,
Triumph o'er splendours of unutterable light
And know supremely this, O God, — Thou art,
Feeling in all this tumult of my soul
Grand kinship with the glory of Thy might.

SEA SONNETS

I

Out with the tide — afar, afar, afar,
Where will the wide dark take us, you and me —
The darkness and the tempest and the sea?
How long we waited where the tall ships are,
Disconsolate and safe within the bar!
Ocean forever calling us, but we —
God, how we stifled there, nor dared be free
With a sharp knife and night and the wild dare!
But now, the hawser cut, adrift, away —
Mad with escape, what care we to what doom
The bitter night may bear us? Lost, alone,
In a vague world of roaring surge astray,
Out with the tide and into the unknown,
Compassed about with rapture and the gloom!

II

We two, waifs, wide-eyed and without fear,
With the dark swirl of life about our prow,
The hollow, heedless swash of year on year
That bears us on and recks not where nor how!
Our skiff is but a feather on the foam,
No mighty galleon strong to meet the storm —
An open boat — God's gift to us for home,
And but each other's arms to keep us warm!
What port for us to make? Our only star
To steer by is the star of missing sails,
Our only haven where the kelpies are —
Yet, you great merchantmen with freighted bales,
Rebel and lost and aimless as we go,
We keep a joy your pride can never know.

III

Moon of my midlight! Moon of the dark sea,
Where like a petrel's ghost my sloop is driven!
Behold, about me and under and over me,
The darkness and the waters and the heaven —
Huge, shapeless monsters as of worlds in birth,
Dragons of Fate, that hold me not in scope —
Bar up my way with fierce, indifferent mirth,
And fall in giant frolic on my hope.

Their next mad rush may whelm me in the wave,
The dreaded horror of the sightless deep —
Only thy love, like moonlight, pours to save
My soul from the despairs that lunge and leap.
Moon of my night, though hell and death assail,
The tremble of thy light is on my sail.

AT A SUMMER RESORT

Miss you so by day, your look, your walk,
The rustle of your draperies on the stair,
Our Leyden-jar-fuls of electric talk,
The sense of you about me everywhere.
The people bore me in the boarding-house,
I hardly can accord them yes or no;
The beauty of the valleys can arouse
No such elation as a year ago.
But when the last dull guest has gone to bed
And only crickets keep me company,
In the mesmeric night when truth is said —
When you, dear loveliness with drooping eye,
Demurely enter through the unreal wall,
And I forget you went away at all.

NEW YORK

The low line of the walls that lie outspread
Miles on long miles, the fog and smoke and slime,
The wharves and ships with flags of every clime,
The domes and steeples rising overhead!
It is not these. Rather it is the tread
Of the million heavy feet that keep sad time
To heavy thoughts, the want that mothers crime,
The weary toiling for a bitter bread,
The perishing of poets for renown,
The shriek of shame from the concealing waves.
Ah, me! how many heart-beats day by day
Go to make up the life of the vast town!
O myriad dead in unremembered graves!
O torrent of the living down Broadway!

A GROTESQUE

Our Gothic minds have gargoyle fancies. Odd,
That there will come a day when you and I
Shall not be you and I, that we shall lie,
We two, in the damp earth-mould, above each clod
A drunken headstone in the neglected sod,
Thereon the phrase, Hic Jacet, worn awry,
And then our virtues, bah! — and piety —
Perhaps some cheeky reference to God!
And haply after many a century
Some spectacled old man shall drive the birds
A moment from their song in the lonely spot
And make a copy of the quaint old words —
They will then be quaint and old — and all for what?
To fill a gap in a genealogy.

WHEN THE PRIEST LEFT

What did he say?
To seek love otherwhere
Nor bind the soul to clay?
It may be so — I cannot tell —
But I know that life is fair,
And love's bold clarion in the air
Outdins his little vesper-bell.

Love God? Can I touch God with both my hands?
Can I breathe in his hair and brush his cheek
He is too far to seek.
If nowhere else be love, who understands
What thing it is?
This love is but a name that wise men speak.
God hath no lips to kiss.

Let God be; surely, if he will,
At the end of days,
He can win love as well as praise.
Why must we spill
The human love out at his feet?
Let be this talk of good and ill!
Though God be God, art thou not fair and sweet?

Open the window; let the air
Blow in on us.
It is enough to find you fair,
To touch with fingers timorous

Your sunlit hair, —
To turn my body to a prayer,
And kiss you — thus.

THE GIFT OF ART

A FRAGMENT

I dreamed that a child was born; and at his birth
The Angel of the Word stood by the hearth
And spake to her that bare him: "Look without!
Behold the beauty of the Day, the shout
Of colour to glad colour, rocks and trees
And sun and sea and wind and sky! All these
Are God's expression, art-work of his hand,
Which men must love ere they may understand,
By which alone he speaks till they have grace
To hear his voice and look upon his face.
For first and last of all things in the heart
Of God as man the glory is of art.
What gift could God bestow or man beseech,
Save spirit unto spirit uttered speech?
Wisdom were not, for God himself could find
No way to reach the unresponsive mind,
Sweet Love were dead, and all the crowded skies
A loneliness and not a Paradise.
Teach the child language, mother..."

TO JAMES WHITCOMB RILEY

Though aiblins some deserve as highly
O' that braw winsome lass an' wily
Wha gi'es a kiss to bardies slyly
An' sets 'em liltin',
I ken there's nane can equal Riley
To 'scape her jiltin'.
How comes it, man, ye ken sae well
The Muse's tricks? Hae yea spell
To keep her sae a' to yoursel',
An' fu' in Fame's e'e?
Fame? — let that hizzie gae to hell!
Here's to you, Jamesie!

TO RUDYARD KIPLING

What need have you of praising? Could I find
Some lonely poet no one praises yet,
Him rather would I choose, that he might know
A fellow-craftsman knew him, marked him, loved.
But you — the whole world praises you. What need
Have you of any speech I have to give?
Yet for the craft's sake I must give you praise;
And for the craft's sake you will pardon me.
But I would rather meet you face to face
And talk of other and indifferent things,
And say no word of all that I would say,
Praise and thanksgiving for your splendid song,
Praise and the pride of the empires of the Blood —
But leave you, silent, as we English do —
And you would know — and you would understand.

ROMANY SIGNS

On the publication of "Patrins," by Louise Imogen Guiney.

If I should wander out some afternoon
About the end of May or early June,
And at a crossroads in the hills discover
A spray of apple or a sprig of clover,

Set for a sign to tell who went that way,
Which road he took and how he fared that day,
"Ho, ho," I'd whistle, "here's a gipsy token,
As plain as if the very word were spoken."

Then down I turn, hot foot, and off I trudge
Hard on his trail, while sceptics mutter, "Fudge!"
They know the way, these travel-wise Egyptians,
And I — enough to follow their inscriptions.

So, bless you! in a mile or two at most,
I've overtaken, almost passed, my host
Camped in the finest grove in all the county
And bidding me to supper on his bounty.

There's nothing like a bit of open sky
To give a touch of poetry to pie;
And here's a poem (call it Sphinx in Myrtle)

Would make an alderman forget his turtle.

Now, there's a Romany in Auburndale,
Wild as a faun and sound as cakes and ale,
One of the tribe of Stevenson and Borrow,
Who live to-day and let alone to-morrow.

(God keeps a few still living in the sun, —
The man who wrote The Seven Seas, for one,
And Island Stoddard, — just to prove the folly
Of smug repose and pious melancholy.)

So when I see her signal in the hedge,
(I mean her new book on the counter's edge,)
"Ho, ho," say I, "that Guiney's broken loose again,
Cut a new quill and put her craft to use again."

Enough for me! I'm off. And, fellows all,
Who could resist the Auburndalean call
To go a-foraging? That's what the spring's for,
What bards have wits and bumblebees have wings for.

I'll warrant here's a road to Arcady
With goodly cheer and merry company,
Skirting the pleasant foot-hills of Philosophy,
Far from the quaggy marshes of Theosophy.

O for the trail, wherever it may lead,
From small credulity to larger creed,
Till we behold this world without detraction
As God did seven times with satisfaction!

THE MAN WITH THE TORTOISE

TO W. M. F.

Such curious things the mind bids stay,
Of the thousand and one that pass it by!
The morning we walked through Paris in May,
If you remember as well as I,

There happened — a nothing — an incident —
One of those trifles that flit half seen,
Save where the spirit sits intent,
Furtive and shy at her window screen.

The servants' gossip of eye and ear
May surge and hum at her door in spring
Of the pageant of beauty drawing near,
But she — she is watching a stranger thing!

The myriad rabble of fact and form
May gleam till the senses dance with glee;
But calm, unmoved as the very norm
And centre of being, muses she;

Indifferent to loveliness, line or hue,
Till a chance bird-wing or a slant sun-ray
May fall as prompt as an actor's cue,
And there is her part. So it was that day.

We had turned from your door in the rue Vignon,
The third on the left from the Madelaine...
Forget it? There's no forgetting when one
Is come at length to his Castle in Spain.

For you were the friend I had loved of old,
And pictured so often in Paris here,
And promised myself some day to hold
Unaltered and safe and sound, no fear.

For our mistress Nature is great and wise,
And the love of her is eternity;
But there comes a day when a man must rise
And go where the heart in him longs to be.

So the sea was crossed, and the hour was come;
It was hand on shoulder with us once more.
There was speech enough though the lips were dumb,
When I stood at last at your modest door.

Your breakfast of capon and Burgundy,
Our talk of Harvard and Norton's fame,
And your friend the Druse, with cigars laid by —
Your gift from the Baroness What's-her-name.

Then into the street of the Capucines
In the blaze of the Paris sun we strolled;
Once more at touch of your blithe light mien
I knew how a springflower breaks the mould.

Through the gay May weather when life was good,
Idly we sauntered from block to block,
Till round a corner appeared, and stood,

A fellow in workman's cap and smock,

Basket on arm and whistling low
To something held in the rough right hand.
A tortoise! Yes, and the creature, so,
Grown tame at the music's soft command,

Emboldened to peep from the safe snug shell,
Had pushed up its head to the whistler's face,
The least of wild things under the spell
Of the last and humblest of Orpheus' race.

A fragment from some Greek Idyllist,
The plain good look of the bolder text,
Preserving for us the colour and gist
Of a simple age and a life unvexed.

Did the beast recall how the syrinx blew
When his father Pan first notched a reed?
Was it some familiar note he knew
In the workman's whistle that made him heed?

Did there wake remembrance dim and large
Of the drench and glamour, the mist and gleam,
Of a morning once by the shining marge
And murmurous run of a Dorian stream?

Or was it only the reedy plash
Of a Norman river, sunny and small,
Where a sound of wind in the scarlet ash,
Blown high, blown low, once held him thrall?

Was there nought but the sweet luxurious thrill
Of the senses, strung to rhythm and time?
No shadow of soul, to remember and fill
The shell that day with a joy sublime?

So still, as for very life he feared
To lose one note of the wild sweet strain.
Ah, mortal, blow till thy breath has cleared
Ages of dust from a haunted brain!

And often I think, as the days go by,
Of our whistling man and the small mute friend
He had charmed. And a scrap of legendry
Has always given the thought a trend.

An Indian myth (you will pardon its worth!)

Says a tortoise, firm in his arching shell,
Upbears the creature that bears the earth;
But what holds the tortoise none can tell.

The tortoise, I venture, may symbolise
The husk of being, the outward world,
The substance of beauty, each form and guise
Where the lurking mind is ensheathed, encurled.

And suppose at the lip of the shell there stood
A mortal bent on the strange and new,
Trying each cadence wild and rude,
Till the magic melody he blew!

What glimpse to that cunning dweller in clay
Might not the old tortoise Earth afford
Of her very self, some morning in May,
Emerged for once to the perfect chord!

THE SCEPTICS

It was the little leaves beside the road.

Said Grass, "What is that sound
So dismally profound,
That detonates and desolates the air?"
"That is St. Peter's bell,"
Said rain-wise Pimpernel;
"He is music to the godly,
Though to us he sounds so oddly,
And he terrifies the faithful unto prayer."

Then something very like a groan
Escaped the naughty little leaves.

Said Grass, "And whither track
These creatures all in black,
So woebegone and penitent and meek?"
"They're mortals bound for church,"
Said the little Silver Birch;
"They hope to get to heaven
And have their sins forgiven,
If they talk to God about it once a week."

And something very like a smile
Ran through the naughty little leaves.

Said Grass, "What is that noise
That startles and destroys
Our blessed summer brooding when we're tired?"
"That's folk a-praising God,"
Said the tough old cynic Clod;
"They do it every Sunday,
They'll be all right on Monday;
It's just a little habit they've acquired."

And laughter spread among the little leaves.

A THANKSGIVING

I thank thee, Earth, for water good,
The sea's great bath of buoyant green
Or the cold mountain torrent's flood,
That I may keep this body clean.

I thank thee more for goodly wine,
That wise as Omar I may be,
Or Horace when he went to dine
With Lydia or with Lalage.

A STACCATO TO O LE LUPE

O Le Lupe, Gelett Burgess, this is very sad to find:
In The Bookman for September, in a manner most unkind,
There appears a half-page picture, makes me think I've lost my mind.

They have reproduced a window, — Doxey's window, — (I dare say
In your rambles you have seen it, passed it twenty times a day,)
As "A Novel Exhibition of Examples of Decay."

There is Nordau we all sneer at, and Verlaine we all adore,
And a little book of verses with its betters by the score,
With three faces on the cover I believe I've seen before.

Well, here's matter for reflection, makes me wonder where I am.
Here is Ibsen the gray lion, linked to Beardsley the black lamb.
I was never out of Boston; all that I can say is, "Damn!"

Who could think, in two short summers we should cause so much remark,
With no purpose but our pastime, and to make the public hark,

When I soloed on The Chap-Book, and you answered with The Lark!

Do young people take much pleasure when they read that sort of thing?
"Well, they buy it," answered Doxey, "and I take what it will bring.
Publishers may dread extinction — not with such fads on the string.

"There is always sale for something, and demand for what is new.
These young men who are so restless, and have nothing else to do,
Like to think there is 'a movement,' just to keep themselves in view.

"There is nothing in Decadence but the magic of a name.
People talk and papers drivel, scent a vice, and hint a shame;
And all that is good for business, helps to boom my little game."

But when I sit down to reason, think to stand upon my nerve,
Meditate on portly leisure with a balance in reserve,
In he comes with his "Decadence!" like a fly in my preserve.

I can see myself, O Burgess, half a century from now,
Laid to rest among the ghostly, like a broken toy somehow,
All my lovely songs and ballads vanished with your "Purple Cow."

But I will return some morning, though I know it will be hard,
To Cornhill among the bookstalls, and surprise some minor bard,
Turning over their old rubbish for the treasures we discard.

I shall warn him like a critic, creeping when his back is turned,
"Ink and paper, dead and done with; Doxey spent what Doxey earned;
Poems doubtless are immortal, where a poem can be discerned!"

How his face will go to ashes, when he feels his empty purse!
How he'll wish his vogue were greater; plume himself it is no worse;
Then go bother the dear public with his puny little verse!

Don't I know how he will pose it; patronize our larger time;
"Poor old Browning; little Kipling; what attempts they made to rhyme!"
Just let me have half an hour with that nincompoop sublime!

I will haunt him like a purpose, I will ghost him like a fear;
When he least expects my presence, I'll be mumbling in his ear,
"O Le Lupe lived in Frisco, and I lived in Boston here.

"Never heard of us? Good heavens, can you never have been told
Of the Larks we used to publish, and theChapbooks that we sold?
Where are all our first editions?" I feel damp and full of mould.

I think it must be spring. I feel
All broken up and thawed.
I'm sick of everybody's "wheel;"
I'm sick of being jawed.

I am too winter-killed to live,
Cold-sour through and through.
O Heavenly Barber, come and give
My soul a dry shampoo!

I'm sick of all these nincompoops,
Who weep through yards of verse,
And all these sonneteering dupes
Who whine and froth and curse.

I'm sick of seeing my own name
Tagged to some paltry line,
While this old corpus without shame
Sits down to meat and wine.

I'm sick of all these Yellow Books,
And all these Bodley Heads;
I'm sick of all these freaks and spooks
And frights in double leads.

When good Napoleon's publisher
Was dangled from a limb,
He should have had an editor
On either side of him.

I'm sick of all this taking on
Under a foreign name;
For when you call it decadent,
It's rotten just the same.

I'm sick of all this puling trash
And namby-pamby rot, —
A Pegasus you have to thrash
To make him even trot!

An Age-end Art! I would not give,
For all their plotless plays,
One round Falstaffian adjective
Or one Miltonic phrase.

I'm sick of all this poppycock

In bilious green and blue;
I'm tired to death of taking stock
Of everything that's "New."

New Art, New Movements, and New Schools,
All maimed and blind and halt!
And all the fads of the New Fools
Who cannot earn their salt.

I'm sick of the New Woman, too.
Good Lord, she's worst of all.
Her rights, her sphere, her point of view,
And all that folderol!

She makes me wish I were the snake
Inside of Eden's wall,
To give the tree another shake,
And see another fall.

I'm very much of Byron's mind;
I like sufficiency;
But just the common garden kind
Is good enough for me.

I want to find a warm beech wood,
And lie down, and keep still;
And swear a little; and feel good;
Then loaf on up the hill,

And let the Spring house-clean my brain,
Where all this stuff is crammed;
And let my heart grow sweet again;
And let the Age be damned.

HER VALENTINE

What, send her a valentine? Never!
I see you don't know who "she" is.
I should ruin my chances forever;
My hopes would collapse with a fizz.

I can't see why she scents such disaster
When I take heart to venture a word;
I've no dream of becoming her master,
I've no notion of being her lord.

All I want is to just be her lover!
She's the most up-to-date of her sex,
And there's such a multitude of her,
No wonder they call her complex.

She's a bachelor, even when married,
She's a vagabond, even when housed;
And if ever her citadel's carried
Her suspicions must not be aroused.

She's erratic, impulsive and human,
And she blunders, — as goddesses can;
But if she's what they call the New Woman,
Then I'd like to be the New Man.

I'm glad she makes books and paints pictures,
And typewrites and hoes her own row,
And it's quite beyond reach of conjectures
How much further she's going to go.

When she scorns, in the L-road, my proffer
Of a seat and hangs on to a strap;
I admire her so much, I could offer
To let her ride up on my lap.

Let her undo the stays of the ages,
That have cramped and confined her so long!
Let her burst through the frail candy cages
That fooled her to think they were strong!

She may enter life's wide vagabondage,
She may do without flutter or frill,
She may take off the chains of her bondage, —
And anything else that she will.

She may take me off, for example,
And she probably does when I'm gone.
I'm aware the occasion is ample;
That's why I so often take on.

I'm so glad she can win her own dollars
And know all the freedom it brings.
I love her in shirt-waists and collars,
I love her in dress-reform things.

I love her in bicycle skirtlings —
Especially when there's a breeze —
I love her in crinklings and quirklings

And anything else that you please.

I dote on her even in bloomers —
If Parisian enough in their style —
In fact, she may choose her costumers,
Wherever her fancy beguile.

She may box, she may shoot, she may wrestle,
She may argue, hold office or vote,
She may engineer turret or trestle,
And build a few ships that will float.

She may lecture (all lectures but curtain)
Make money, and naturally spend,
If I let her have her way, I'm certain
She'll let me have mine in the end!

IN PHILISTIA

Of all the places on the map,
Some queer and others queerer,
Arcadia is dear to me,
Philistia is dearer.

There dwell the few who never knew
The pangs of heavenly hunger,
As fresh and fair and fond and frail
As when the world was younger.

If there is any sweeter sound
Than bobolinks or thrushes,
It is the frou-frou of their silks —
The roll of their barouches.

I love them even when they're good,
As well as when they're sinners —
When they are sad and worldly wise
And when they are beginners.

(I say I do; of course the fact,
For better or for worse, is,
My unerratic life denies
My too erotic verses.)

I dote upon their waywardness,
Their foibles and their follies.

If there's a madder pate than Di's,
Perhaps it may be Dolly's.

They have no "problems" to discuss,
No "theories" to discover;
They are not "new"; and I — I am
Their very grateful lover.

I care not if their minds confuse
Alastor with Aladdin;
And Cimabue is far less
To them than Chimmie Fadden.

They never heard of William Blake,
Nor saw a Botticelli;
Yet one is, "Yours till death, Louise,"
And one, "Your loving Nelly."

They never tease me for my views,
Nor tax me with my grammar;
Nor test me on the latest news,
Until I have to stammer.

They never talk about their "moods,"
They never know they have them;
The world is good enough for them,
And that is why I love them.

They never puzzle me with Greek,
Nor drive me mad with Ibsen;
Yet over forms as fair as Eve's
They wear the gowns of Gibson.

PEACE

There is peace, you say. I believe you. Peace? Ay, we know it well —
Not the peace of the smile of God, but the peace of the leer of Hell,
Peace, that the rich may fatten and barter their souls for gain,
Peace, that the hungry may slay and rob the corpse of the slain,
Peace, that the heart of the people may rot with a vile gangrene.
What though the men are bloodless! What's a man to a machine?

Here you come with your Economics. If ever the Devil designed
A science, 'twas yours, I doubt not, a study to Hell's own mind,
Merciless, soulless, sordid, the science of selfish greed,
Blind to the light of wisdom, and deaf to the voice of need.

And you prate of the wealth of nations, as if it were bought and sold!
The wealth of nations is men, not silk and cotton and gold.

How will you measure in money the cost of knowledge and Art?
Is honour valued in bank-notes? Can you pay for a broken heart?
Can you reckon the worth of a poem by a standard of meat and drink?
Can you buy with gold and silver a heart too great to shrink?
Tell me, how many dollars will pay for the lifeblood shed
From the veins of the true and valiant who feared not and are dead?

Battle is fearful — I grant it. The fields are burnt bare with its breath,
Death and the wrongs of women that cry out louder than death,
The grime and the trampled faces and the shrieking of shells in the air,
White lips of victims that pray and there comes no help for their prayer,
And Famine that follows the armies, and Crime that skulks in their rear,—
These are fearful alike to the soldiers that strike and the cravens that fear.

But there's yet one woe far worse than war with its griefs and graves —
To sink to a nation of cowards, sycophants, thieves and slaves,
There is one thing for man or nation more within man's control
And worse than the death of the body, and that is the death of the soul.
But the sins of the city are silent and her ruin is wrought by stealth
And the sores that fester are cloaked and her rottenness masks as health.

True Peace is a holy thing — the peace God gives to his own,
Heart's peace, though the body move where the thickest shot is thrown,
Deeps of peace forever unplumbed by a mortal eye —
But the peace of the world is the Devil's, a mockery and a lie,
Better city arrayed against city and hamlet with hamlet at strife,
So valour outvalue lucre and honour be more than life.

A LYRIC

From the French of Maurice Maeterlinck.

And if some day he come back,
What should he be told? —
Tell him he was waited for,
Till my heart was cold.

And if he ask me yet again,
Not recognizing me? —
Speak him fair and sisterly;
His heart breaks, maybe.

And if he ask me where you are,

What shall I reply? —
Give him my golden ring,
And make no reply.

And if he ask me why the hall
Is left desolate? —
Show him the unlit lamp
And the open gate.

And if he should ask me, then,
How you fell asleep? —
Tell him that I smiled, for fear
Lest he should weep.

THE LOST COMRADE

Now who will tell me aright
The way my lost companion went in the night?
My vanished comrade who passed from the roofs of men,
And will not come again.

I have wandered up and down
Through all the streets of this bright and busy town,
Yet no one has seen a trace of him since the day
He silently went away.

I have haunted the wharves and the slips,
And talked with foreigners from the incoming ships;
But when I questioned them closely about my friend,
They seemed not to comprehend.

From men of book-learning, too,
I have sought knowledge, confident that they knew;
But when I inquired simply about my chum,
They glanced at me and were dumb.

I have entered your churches of stone,
And heard discourse about God and the throng round his throne;
But the preacher knew nothing at all, when I broke in with, "Where?"
And the people could only stare.

Ah, no, you may read and read,
Pile modern heresy upon ancient creed!
But for all your study you know no more than I,
Under the open sky.

So 't is, Back to the Inn! for me,
Where my great friend and I were happy and free.
And I will remember his beautiful words and his ways,
For the rest of my days.

How eager he was for truth,
Yet never scorned the good things of his youth,
The soul of gentleness and the soul of love!
I shall be wise enough.

TEN COMMANDMENTS

It is right:

I. LOVE
To love everybody a little and some people a great deal.

II. FAITH
To trust the God who made us is good and will not forget us.

III. OBEDIENCE
To obey those who have the right to hold themselves responsible for us.

IV. HOPE
To look on the bright side of things and keep a good heart up.

V. COURAGE
To dare do whatever we think we ought to do.

VI. CHEERFULNESS
To express our good, happy feelings, not the others.

VII. PRUDENCE
To use our intelligence to avoid trouble.

It is wrong:

VIII
To hate or hurt any one, except for a greater good; to be mean and selfish; to be unjust.

IX
To tell lies, except when people ask what they have no right to know.

X
To do anything dirty, or ugly, or intemperate.

QUATRAINS

I

Life as it is! Accept it; it is thine!
The God that gave it, gave it for thy good.
The God that made it had not been divine
Could he have set thee poison for thy food.

II

Abstain not; Life and Love, like night and day,
Offer themselves to us on their own terms,
— Not ours. Accept their bounty while ye may,
Before we be accepted by the worms.

III

We rail at Time and Chance, and break our hearts
To make the glory of to-day endure.
Is the sun dead because the day departs?
And are the suns of Life and Love less sure?

IV

Fear not the menace of the bye-and-bye.
To-day is ours; to-morrow Fate must give.
Stretch out your hands and eat, although ye die!
Better to die than never once to live.

THE ADVENTURERS

We are adventurers who come
Before the merchants and the priests;
Our only legacy from home,
A wisdom older than the East's.

Soldiers of Fortune, we unfurl
The banners of a forlorn hope,
Leaving the city smoke to curl
O'er dingy roofs where puppets mope.

We are the Ishmaelites of earth
Who at the crossroads beat the drum;
None guess our lineage nor our birth,
The flag we serve nor whence we come.

We claim a Sire that no man knows,
The Emperor of Nights and Days,
Who saith to Caesar, "Go," — he goes,
'To Alexander, "Stay," — he stays.

Out of a greater town than Tyre,
We march to conquer and control
The golden hill-lands of Desire,
The Nicaraguas of the soul.

We have cast in our lot with Truth;
We will not flinch nor stay the hand,
Till on the last skyline of youth
We look down on his fair new land.

We put from port without a fear,
For Freedom on this Spanish Main;
And the great wind that bore us here
Will drive our galleys home again.

If not, we can lie down and die,
Content to perish with our peers,
So one more rood we gained thereby
For Love's Dominion through the years.

Bliss Carman - An Appreciation

How many Canadians—how many even among the few who seek to keep themselves informed of the best in contemporary literature, who are ever on the alert for the new voices—realise, or even suspect, that this Northern land of theirs has produced a poet of whom it may be affirmed with confidence and assurance that he is of the great succession of English poets? Yet such—strange and unbelievable though it may seem—is in very truth the case, that poet being (to give him his full name) William Bliss Carman. Canada has full right to be proud of her poets, a small body though they are; but not only does Mr. Carman stand high and clear above them all—his place (and time cannot but confirm and justify the assertion) is among those men whose poetry is the shining glory of that great English literature which is our common heritage.

If any should ask why, if what has been just said is so, there has been—as must be admitted—no general recognition of the fact in the poet's home land, I would answer that there are various and plausible, if not good, reasons for it.

First of all, the poet, as thousands more of our young men of ambition and confidence have done, went early to the United States, and until recently, except for rare and brief visits to his old home down by the sea, has never returned to Canada—though for all that, I am able to state, on his own authority, he is still a Canadian citizen. Then all his books have had their original publication in the United States, and while a few of them have subsequently carried the imprints of Canadian publishers, none of these can be said ever to have made any special effort to push their sale. Another reason for the fact above mentioned is that Mr. Carman has always scorned to advertise himself, while his work has never been the subject of the log-rolling and booming which the work of many another poet has had—to his ultimate loss. A further reason is that he follows a rule of his own in preparing his books for publication. Most poets publish a volume of their work as soon as, through their industry and perseverance, they have material enough on hand to make publication desirable in their eyes. Not so with Mr. Carman, however, his rule being not to publish until he has done sufficient work of a certain general character or key to make a volume. As a result, you cannot fully know or estimate his work by one book, or two books, or even half a dozen; you must possess or be familiar with every one of the score and more volumes which contain his output of poetry before you can realise how great and how many-sided is his genius.

It is a common remark on the part of those who respond readily to the vigorous work of Kipling, or Masefield, even our own Service, that Bliss Carman's poetry has no relation to or concern with ordinary, everyday life. One would suppose that most persons who cared for poetry at all turned to it as a relief from or counter to the burdens and vexations of the daily round; but in any event, the remark referred to seems to me to indicate either the most casual acquaintance with Mr. Carman's work, or a complete misunderstanding and misapprehension of the meaning of it. I grant that you will find little or nothing in it all to remind you of the grim realities and vexing social problems of this modern existence of ours; but to say or to suggest that these things do not exist for Mr. Carman is to say or to suggest something which is the reverse of true. The truth is, he is aware of them as only one with the sensitive organism of a poet can be; but he does not feel that he has a call or mission to remedy them, and still less to sing of them. He therefore leaves the immediate problems of the day to those who choose, or are led, to occupy themselves therewith, and turns resolutely away to dwell upon those things which for him possess infinitely greater importance.

"What are they?" one who knows Mr. Carman only as, say, a lyrist of spring or as a singer of the delights of vagabondia probably will ask in some wonder. Well, the things which concern him above all, I would answer, are first, and naturally, the beauty and wonder of this world of ours, and next the mystery of the earthly pilgrimage of the human soul out of eternity and back into it again.

The poems in the present volume—which, by the way, can boast the high honor of being the very first regular Canadian edition of his work—will be evidence ample and conclusive to every reader, I am sure, of the place which

The perennial enchanted
Lovely world and all its lore

occupy in the heart and soul of Bliss Carman, as well as of the magical power with which he is able to convey the deep and unfailing satisfaction and delight which they possess for him. They, however, represent his latest period (he has had three well-defined periods), comprising selections from three of his last published volumes: The Rough Rider, Echoes from Vagabondia, and April Airs, together with a number of new poems, and do not show, except here and there and by hints and flashes, how great is his preoccupation with the problem of man's existence—

—the hidden import
Of man's eternal plight.

This is manifest most in certain of his earlier books, for in these he turns and returns to the greatest of all the problems of man almost constantly, probing, with consummate and almost unrivalled use of the art of expression, for the secret which surely, he clearly feels, lies hidden somewhere, to be discovered if one could but pierce deeply enough. Pick up Behind the Arras, and as you turn over page after page you cannot but observe how incessantly the poet's mind—like the minds of his two great masters, Browning and Whitman—works at this problem. In "Behind the Arras," the title poem; "In the Wings," "The Crimson House," "The Lodger," "Beyond the Gamut," "The Juggler"—yes, in every poem in the book—he takes up and handles the strange thing we know as, or call, life, turning it now this way, now that, in an effort to find out its meaning and purpose. He comes but little nearer success in this than do most of the rest of men, of course; but the magical and ever-fresh beauty of his expression, the haunting melody of his lines, the variety of his images and figures and the depth and range of his thought, put his searchings and ponderings in a class by themselves.

Lengthy quotation from Mr. Carman's books is not permitted here, and I must guide myself accordingly, though with reluctance, because I believe that in a study such as this the subject should be allowed to speak for himself as much as possible. In "Behind the Arras" the poet describes the passage from life to death as

A cadence dying down unto its source
In music's course,

and goes on to speak of death as

—the broken rhythm of thought and man,
The sweep and span
Of memory and hope
About the orbit where they still must grope
For wider scope,

To be through thousand springs restored, renewed,
With love imbrued,
With increments of will
Made strong, perceiving unattainment still
From each new skill.

Now follow some verses from "Behind the Gamut," to my mind the poet's greatest single achievement;

As fine sand spread on a disc of silver,
At some chord which bids the motes combine,
Heeding the hidden and reverberant impulse,
Shifts and dances into curve and line,

The round earth, too, haply, like a dust-mote,
Was set whirling her assigned sure way,
Round this little orb of her ecliptic
To some harmony she must obey.

And what of man?

Linked to all his half-accomplished fellows,
Through unfrontiered provinces to range—
Man is but the morning dream of nature,
Roused to some wild cadence weird and strange.

Here, now, are some verses from "Pulvis et Umbra," which is to be found in Mr. Carman's first book, Low Tide on Grand Pré, and in which the poet addresses a moth which a storm has blown into his window:

For man walks the world with mourning
Down to death and leaves no trace,
With the dust upon his forehead,
And the shadow on his face.

Pillared dust and fleeing shadow
As the roadside wind goes by,
And the fourscore years that vanish
In the twinkling of an eye.

"Pillared dust and fleeing shadow." Where in all our English literature will one find the life history of man summed up more briefly and, at the same time, more beautifully, than in that wonderful line? Now follows a companion verse to those just quoted, taken from "Lord of My Heart's Elation," which stands in the forefront of From the Green Book of the Bards. It may be remarked here that while the poet recurs again and again to some favorite thought or idea, it is never in the same words. His expression is always new and fresh, showing how deep and true is his inspiration. Again it is man who is pictured:

A fleet and shadowy column
Of dust and mountain rain,
To walk the earth a moment
And be dissolved again.

But while Mr. Carman's speculations upon life's meaning and the mystery of the future cannot but appeal to the thoughtful-minded, it is as an interpreter of nature that he makes his widest appeal. Bliss Carman, I must say here, and emphatically, is no mere landscape-painter; he never, or scarcely ever, paints a picture of nature for its own sake. He goes beyond the outward aspect of things and interprets or translates for us with less keen senses as only a poet whose feeling for nature is of the deepest and profoundest, who has gone to her whole-heartedly and been taken close to her warm bosom, can do. Is this not evident from these verses from "The Great Return"—originally called "The Pagan's Prayer," and for some inscrutable reason to be found only in the limited Collected Poems, issued in two stately volumes in 1905.

When I have lifted up my heart to thee,

Thou hast ever hearkened and drawn near,
And bowed thy shining face close over me,
Till I could hear thee as the hill-flowers hear.

When I have cried to thee in lonely need,
Being but a child of thine bereft and wrung,
Then all the rivers in the hills gave heed;
And the great hill-winds in thy holy tongue—

That ancient incommunicable speech—
The April stars and autumn sunsets know—
Soothed me and calmed with solace beyond reach
Of human ken, mysterious and low.

Who can read or listen to those moving lines without feeling that Mr. Carman is in very truth a poet of nature—nay, Nature's own poet? But how could he be other when, in "The Breath of the Reed" (From the Green Book of the Bards), he makes the appeal?

Make me thy priest, O Mother,
And prophet of thy mood,
With all the forest wonder
Enraptured and imbued.

As becomes such a poet, and particularly a poet whose birth-month is April, Mr. Carman sings much of the early spring. Again and again he takes up his woodland pipe, and lo! Pan himself and all his train troop joyously before us. Yet the singer's notes for all his singing never become wearied or strident; his airs are ever new and fresh; his latest songs are no less spontaneous and winning than were his first, written how many years ago, while at the same time they have gained in beauty and melody. What heart will not stir to the vibrant music of his immortal "Spring Song," which was originally published in the first Songs from Vagabondia, and the opening verses of which follow?

Make me over, mother April,
When the sap begins to stir!
When thy flowery hand delivers
All the mountain-prisoned rivers,
And thy great heart beats and quivers
To revive the days that were,
Make me over, mother April,
When the sap begins to stir!

Take my dust and all my dreaming,
Count my heart-beats one by one,
Send them where the winters perish;
Then some golden noon recherish
And restore them in the sun,
Flower and scent and dust and dreaming,
With their heart-beats every one!

That poem is sufficient in itself to prove that Bliss Carman has full right and title to be called Spring's own lyrist, though it may be remarked here that not all his spring poems are so unfeignedly joyous. Many of them indeed, have a touch, or more than a touch, of wistfulness, for the poet knows well that sorrow lurks under all joy, deep and well hidden though it may be.

Mr. Carman sings equally finely, though perhaps not so frequently, of summer and the other seasons; but as he has other claims upon our attention, I shall forbear to labor the fact, particularly as the following collection demonstrates it sufficiently. One of those other claims is as a writer of sea poetry. Few poets, it may be said, have pictured the majesty and the mystery, the beauty and the terror of the sea, better than he. His Ballads of Lost Haven is a veritable treasure-house for those whose spirits find kinship in wide expanses of moving waters. One of the best known poems in this volume is "The Gravedigger," which opens thus:

Oh, the shambling sea is a sexton old,
And well his work is done.
With an equal grave for lord and knave,
He buries them every one.

Then hoy and rip, with a rolling hip,
He makes for the nearest shore;
And God, who sent him a thousand ship,
Will send him a thousand more;
But some he'll save for a bleaching grave,
And shoulder them in to shore—
Shoulder them in, shoulder them in,
Shoulder them in to shore.

In "The City of the Sea" (Last Songs from Vagabondia) Mr. Carman speaks of the seabells sounding

The eternal cadence of sea sorrow
For Man's lot and immemorial wrong—
The lost strains that haunt the human dwelling
With the ghost of song.

Elsewhere he speaks of

The great sea, mystic and musical.

And here from another poem is a striking picture:

... the old sea
Seems to whimper and deplore
Mourning like a childless crone
With her sorrow left alone—
The eternal human cry
To the heedless passer-by.

I have said above that Mr. Carman has had three distinct periods, and intimated that the poems in the following collection are of his third period. The first period may be said to be represented by the Low Tide and Behind the Arras volumes, while the second is displayed in the three volumes of Songs from Vagabondia, which he published in association with his friend Richard Hovey. Bliss Carman was from the first too original and individual a poet to be directly influenced by anyone else; but there can be no doubt that his friendship with Hovey helped to turn him from over-preoccupation with mysteries which, for all their greatness, are not for man to solve, to an intenser realisation of the beauty and loveliness of the world about him and of the joys of human fellowship. The result is seen in such poems as "Spring Song," quoted in part above, and his perhaps equally well-known "The Joys of the Road," which appeared in the same volume with that poem, and a few verses from which follow:

Now the joys of the road are chiefly these:
A crimson touch on the hardwood trees;

A vagrant's morning wide and blue,
In early fall, when the wind walks, too;

A shadowy highway cool and brown,
Alluring up and enticing down

From rippled waters and dappled swamp,
From purple glory to scarlet pomp;

The outward eye, the quiet will,
And the striding heart from hill to hill.

Some of the finest of arman's work is contained in his elegiac or memorial poems, in which he commemorates Keats, Shelley, William Blake, Lincoln, Stevenson, and other men for whom he has a kindred feeling, and also friends whom he has loved and lost. Listen to these moving lines from "Non Omnis Moriar," written in memory of Gleeson White, and to be found in Last Songs from Vagabondia:

There is a part of me that knows,
Beneath incertitude and fear,
I shall not perish when I pass
Beyond mortality's frontier;

But greatly having joyed and grieved,
Greatly content, shall hear the sigh
Of the strange wind across the lone
Bright lands of taciturnity.

In patience therefore I await
My friend's unchanged benign regard,—
Some April when I too shall be
Spilt water from a broken shard.

In "The White Gull," written for the centenary of the birth of Shelley in 1892, and included in By the Aurelian Wall, he thus apostrophizes that clear and shining spirit:

O captain of the rebel host,
Lead forth and far!
Thy toiling troopers of the night
Press on the unavailing fight;
The sombre field is not yet lost,
With thee for star.

Thy lips have set the hail and haste
Of clarions free
To bugle down the wintry verge
Of time forever, where the surge
Thunders and trembles on a waste
And open sea.

In "A Seamark," a threnody for Robert Louis Stevenson, which appears in the same volume, the poet hails "R.L.S." (of whose tribe he may be said to be truly one) as

The master of the roving kind,

and goes on:

O all you hearts about the world
In whom the truant gypsy blood,
Under the frost of this pale time,
Sleeps like the daring sap and flood
That dreams of April and reprieve!
You whom the haunted vision drives,
Incredulous of home and ease.
Perfection's lovers all your lives!

You whom the wander-spirit loves
To lead by some forgotten clue
Forever vanishing beyond
Horizon brinks forever new;
Our restless loved adventurer,
On secret orders come to him,
Has slipped his cable, cleared the reef,
And melted on the white sea-rim.

"Perfection's lovers all your lives." Of these, it may be said without qualification, is Bliss Carman himself.

No summary of Mr. Carman's work, however cursory, would be worthy of the name if it omitted mention of his ventures in the realm of Greek myth. From the Book of Myths is made up of work of that sort, every poem in it being full of the beauty of phrase and melody of which Mr. Carman alone has the secret. The finest poems in the book, barring the opening one, "Overlord," are "Daphne," "The Dead Faun," "Hylas," and "At Phædra's Tomb," but I can do no more here than name them, for extracts would fail to reveal their full beauty. And beauty, after all is said, is the first and last thing with Mr. Carman. As he says himself somewhere:

The joy of the hand that hews for beauty
Is the dearest solace under the sun.

And again

The eternal slaves of beauty
Are the masters of the world.

A slave—a happy, willing slave—to beauty is the poet himself, and the world can never repay him for the message of beauty which he has brought it.

Kindred to From the Book of Myths, but much more important, is Sappho: One Hundred Lyrics, one of the most successful of the numerous attempts which have been made to recapture the poems by that high priestess of song which remain to us only in fragments. Mr. Carman, as Charles G. D. Roberts points out in an introduction to the volume, has made no attempt here at translation or paraphrasing; his venture has been "the most perilous and most alluring in the whole field of poetry"—that of imaginative and, at the same time, interpretive construction. Brief quotation again would fail to convey an adequate idea of the exquisiteness of the work, and all I can do, therefore, is to urge all lovers of real poetry to possess themselves of Sappho: One Hundred Lyrics, for it is literally a storehouse of lyric beauty.

I must not fail here to speak of From the Book of Valentines, which contains some lovely things, notably "At the Great Release." This is not only one of the finest of all Mr. Carman's poems, but it is also one of the finest poems of our time. It is a love poem, and no one possessing any real feeling for poetry can read it without experiencing that strange thrill of the spirit which only the highest form of poetry can communicate. "Morning and Evening," "In an Iris Meadow," and "A letter from Lesbos" must be also mentioned. In the last named poem, Sappho is represented as writing to Gorgo, and expresses herself in these moving words:

If the high gods in that triumphant time
Have calendared no day for thee to come
Light-hearted to this doorway as of old,
Unmoved I shall behold their pomps go by—
The painted seasons in their pageantry,
The silvery progressions of the moon,
And all their infinite ardors unsubdued,
Pass with the wind replenishing the earth

Incredulous forever I must live
And, once thy lover, without joy behold,
The gradual uncounted years go by,
Sharing the bitterness of all things made.

Mention must be now made of Songs of the Sea Children, which can be described only as a collection of the sweetest and tenderest love lyrics written in our time—

—the lyric songs
The earthborn children sing,
When wild-wood laughter throngs
The shy bird-throats of spring;
When there's not a joy of the heart
But flies like a flag unfurled,
And the swelling buds bring back
The April of the world.

So perfect and complete are these lyrics that it would be almost sacrilege to quote any of them unless entire. Listen however, to these verses:

The day is lost without thee,
The night has not a star.
Thy going is an empty room
Whose door is left ajar.

Depart: it is the footfall
Of twilight on the hills.
Return: and every rood of ground
Breaks into daffodils.

There are those who will have it that Bliss Carman has been away from Canada so long that he has ceased to be, in a real sense, a Canadian. Such assume rather than know, for a very little study of his work would show them that it is shot through and through with the poet's feeling for the land of his birth. Memories of his childhood and youthful years down by the sea are still fresh in Mr. Carman's mind, and inspire him again and again in his writing. "A Remembrance," at the beginning of the present collection, may be pointed to as a striking instance of this, but proof positive is the volume, Songs from a Northern Garden, for it could have been written only by a Canadian, born and bred, one whose heart and soul thrill to the thought of Canada. I would single out from this volume for special mention as being "Canadian" in the fullest sense "In a Grand Pré Garden," "The Keeper's Silence," "At Home and Abroad," "Killoleet," and "Above the Gaspereau," but have no space to quote from them.

But Mr. Carman is not only a Canadian, he is also a Briton; and evidence of this is his Ode on the Coronation, written on the occasion of the crowning of King Edward VII in 1902. This poem—the very existence of which is hardly known among us—ought to be put in the hands of every child and youth who speaks the English tongue, for no other, I dare maintain—nothing by Kipling, or Newbolt, or any other of our so-called "Imperial singers"—expresses more truly and more movingly the deep feeling of love and reverence which the very thought of England evokes in every son of hers, even though it may never have been his to see her white cliffs rise or to tread her storied ground:

O England, little mother by the sleepless Northern tide,
Having bred so many nations to devotion, trust, and pride,
Very tenderly we turn
With welling hearts that yearn
Still to love you and defend you,—let the sons of men discern
Wherein your right and title, might and majesty, reside.

In concluding this, I greatly fear, lamentably inadequate study, I come to the collection which follows, and which, as intimated above, represents the work of Mr. Carman's latest period. I must say at once that, while I yield to no one in admiration for Low Tide and the other books of that period, or for the work of the second period, as represented by the Songs from Vagabondia volumes, I have no hesitation in declaring that I regard the poet's work of the past few years with even higher admiration. It may not possess the force and vigor of the work which preceded it; but anything seemingly missing in that respect is more than made up for me by increased beauty and clarity of expression. The mysticism—verging, or more than verging, at times on symbolism—which marked his earlier poems, and which hung, as it were, as a veil between them and the reader, has gone, and the poet's thought or theme now lies clearly before us as in a mirror. What—to take a verse from the following pages at random—could be more pellucid, more crystal clear in expression—what indeed, could come closer to that achieving of the impossible at which every real poet must aim—than this from "In Gold Lacquer".

Gold are the great trees overhead,
And gold the leaf-strewn grass,
As though a cloth of gold were spread
To let a seraph pass.
And where the pageant should go by,
Meadow and wood and stream,
The world is all of lacquered gold,
Expectant as a dream.

The poet, happily, has fully recovered from the serious illness which laid him low some two years ago, and which for a time caused his friends and admirers the gravest concern, and so we may look forward hopefully to seeing further volumes of verse come from the press to make certain his name and fame. But if, for any reason, this should not be—which the gods forfend!—Later Poems, I dare affirm, must and will be regarded as the fine flower and crowning achievement of the genius and art of Bliss Carman.

R. H. HATHAWAY.
Toronto, 1921.

Bliss Carman – A Short Biography

William Bliss Carman was born in Fredericton, in New Brunswick on April 15th 1861. 'Bliss' was his mother's maiden name. She was descended from Daniel Bliss of Concord, Massachusetts, who was the great-grandfather to Ralph Waldo Emerson.

Carman was educated at Fredericton Collegiate School. Here, under the influence of the headmaster George Robert Parkin, he gained an appreciation of classical literature and was introduced to the poetry of many of the Pre-Raphaelites especially Dante Gabriel Rossetti and Algernon Charles Swinburne.

From here he graduated to the University of New Brunswick, obtaining his B.A. there in 1881. As is common with so many writers his first published piece was for the University magazine and for Carman that was in 1879.

England now beckoned and he spent a year at Oxford and then the University of Edinburgh (1882–1883). He returned home to Canada to work on his M.A. which he obtained from the University of New Brunswick in 1884.

Tragically his father died in January, 1885, followed by his mother in February of the following year. Carman now enrolled in Harvard University for a year. There he met and was part of a literary circle that included the American poet Richard Hovey, who would become his close friend, and later collaborator, on the successful Vagabondia poetry series. Carman and Hovey were members of the "Visionists" circle along with Herbert Copeland and F. Holland Day, who would later form the Boston publishing firm Copeland & Day and, in turn, launch Vagabondia.

After Harvard Carman briefly returned to Canada, but was back in Boston by February of 1890 saying "Boston is one of the few places where my critical education and tastes could be of any use to me in earning money. New York and London are about the only other places." However, he was unable to find work in Boston but was more successful in New York becoming the literary editor of the semi-religious New York Independent. There he helped Canadian poets get published and introduced them to a wider readership than they could receive in Canada.

However, Carman and work as an editor were not destined for a long career together and he was dismissed in 1892. There followed short stays with Current Literature, Cosmopolitan, The Chap-Book, and The Atlantic Monthly. Whilst these appointments provided the basis for a career and an income he was not suited to their demands. From 1895 he would only work as a contributor to magazines and newspapers whilst he worked on his volumes of poetry.

Carman first published a book of poetry in 1893 with Low Tide on Grand Pré. He had written the title poem in the summer of 1886 and it had (whilst he was still at Harvard) been published in the spring of 1887 by Atlantic Monthly. Despite its critical acceptance there was no Canadian company prepared to publish the volume. When an American company did so it went bankrupt. Life was becoming difficult for the young poet.

The following year was decidedly better. His partnership with Richard Hovey had given birth to Songs of Vagabondia and it was published by their friends at Copeland & Day. It was an immediate success. The young men were delighted at such a reception. It quickly sold out and was re-printed a number of times. Although these re-prints were small (usually 500-1000 copies) they were frequent.

On the back of this success they would write a further three volumes, which in their turn were almost as successful. They quickly became the center of a cult following, especially among students who empathized with the poetry's anti-materialistic themes, its celebration of personal freedom, and its glorification of comradeship."

The success of Songs of Vagabondia prompted the Boston firm, Stone & Kimball, to reissue Low Tide on Grand Pré and to hire Carman as the editor of its literary journal, The Chapbook. This ceased after a year when the company relocated and Carman expressed his desire to remain in Boston.

In 1885 Carman brought out Behind the Arras, a somewhat more serious and philosophical work centered on the premise of a long meditation using the speaker's house and its many rooms as a symbol of life and the choices to be made. However, the idea and its execution did not quite meld.

Signficantly, in 1896, Carman met Mrs Mary Perry King, who rapidly became patron, adviser and sometime lover. She put money in his pocket, and food in his mouth and, when he struck bottom, often repaired his confidence as well as helping to sell the work. She also later became his writing collaborator on two verse dramas.

Mitchell Kennerley, Carman's roommate wrote that, "On the rare occasions they had intimate relations they always advised me of by leaving a bunch of violets — Mary favorite flower — on the pillow of my bed." If her husband, Dr. King, knew of this arrangement he seems not to have objected. He was a great supporter of Carman's career and seemingly his wife's complicated involvement with that.

In 1897 Carman published Ballad of Lost Haven, a collection of poetry about the sea. Its notable poems include the macabre sea shanty, The Gravedigger. The following year, 1898, came By the Aurelian Wall, the title poem itself was an elegy to John Keats and the book a collection of formal elegies.

In 1899 his publisher, Lamson, Wolffe was taken over by the Boston firm of Small, Maynard & Co., who had also acquired the rights to Low Tide on Grand Pré. The copyrights to of his books were now held by one publisher and, in lieu of earnings, Carman took what would ultimately be a disastrous financial stake in the company.

As the century turned Carman was hard at work on what would eventually be a five-volume set of poetry; "Pans Pipes". Pan, the goat-god, was traditionally associated with poetry and the coming together of the earthly and the divine. The five volumes were all published between 1902 – 1905.

The inspiration for this came from Mary who had persuaded Carman to write in both prose and poetry about the ideas of 'unitrinianism.' This drew on the theories of François-Alexandre-Nicolas-Chéri Delsarte and was defined as a strategy of mind-body-spirit harmonization aimed at undoing the physical, psychological, and spiritual damage caused by urban modernity. The definition may be rather woolly but for Carman it resulted in some very fine work across the five-volume series. This shared belief between Mary and Carman created a further bond but did isolate him from his circle of friends.

The excellence of a number of these poems did much to install Carman as the most noted of Canadian Poets and eventually their own Poet Laureate. Among the most often quoted and printed are "The Dead Faun" (from Volume I), "Lord of My Heart's Elation" (Volume II) and many of the erotic poems from Volume III.

In the middle of publication in 1903, Small, Maynard failed and with it went all the assets Carman had tied up in the company.

Carman immediately signed with another Boston publisher, L.C. Page, who would publish seven new books of Carman poetry in this hectic period up to 1905. They released a further three books based on Carman's Transcript columns, and a prose work on Unitrinianism, The Making of Personality, that he'd written with Mary King.

Carman now felt secure enough to pursue his 'dream project,' namely a deluxe edition of his collected poetry to 1903. Page acquired the distribution rights on the condition that the book be sold privately, by subscription. Unfortunately, the demand wasn't there and it failed. Carman was deeply disappointed and lost faith in Page. However, their grip on his copyrights was absolute and sadly no further collected editions were to be published during his lifetime.

By 1904 his income was restricted and the offer to be editor-in-chief of the 10-volume project, The World's Best Poetry, was eagerly accepted.

For Carman perhaps his best years as a poet were now behind him. From 1908 he lived near the Kings' New Canaan, Connecticut, estate, that he named "Sunshine", or in the summer in a cabin in the Catskills, which he called "Moonshine."

With Literary tastes now moving away from what he could provide his income further dwindled and his health started to deteriorate.

In 1912 Carman published the final work in the Vagabondia series. Richard Hovey had died in 1900 and so this last work was purely his. It has a distinct elegiac tone as if remembering the past works themselves.

Although Carman was not politically active he did campaign during the World War One, as a member of the Vigilantes, who supported the American entry into the titanic struggle on the Allied side.

By 1920, Carman was impoverished and recovering from a near-fatal attack of tuberculosis. He returned to Canada and began to undertake a series of publicly successful and somewhat lucrative reading tours, saying "there is nothing worth talking of in book sales compared with reading. Breathless attention, crowded halls, and a strange, profound enthusiasm such as I never guessed could be,' he reported to a friend. 'And good thrifty money too. Think of it! An entirely new life for me, and I am the most surprised person in Canada.'"

On October 28th, 1921 Carman was honored at a dinner held by the newly-formed Canadian Authors' Association, at the Ritz Carlton Hotel in Montreal, where he was crowned Canada's Poet Laureate with a wreath of maple leaves.

Carman is placed among the Confederation Poets, a group that included his cousin, Charles G.D. Roberts, Archibald Lampman, and Duncan Campbell Scott. Carman was perhaps the best and is credited with the widest recognition. However, whilst the others carefully supplemented their income with writing novels and works for the magazines, or even other careers, Carman only wrote poetry together with a small amount of writing on literary ideas, philosophy, and aesthetics.

He continued his reading tours, and by 1925 had finally secured a new Canadian publisher; McClelland & Stewart (Toronto), who issued a collection of selected earlier verse and would now became his main publisher. Although they benefited from Carman's increased popularity and his revered position in Canadian literature, his former publisher L.C. Page would not relinquish its copyrights to his earlier works.

In his last years, Carman was a member of the Halifax literary and social set, The Song Fishermen and in 1927 he edited The Oxford Book of American Verse.

William Bliss Carman died of a brain hemorrhage, at the age of 68, in New Canaan on the 8th June, 1929. He was cremated in New Canaan and his ashes interred at Forest Hill Cemetery, Fredericton, with a national memorial service held at the Anglican cathedral there.

It was only a quarter of a century later, on May 13th, 1954, that a scarlet maple tree was planted at his graveside, to honour his request in the 1892 poem "The Grave-Tree":

Let me have a scarlet maple
For the grave-tree at my head,
With the quiet sun behind it,
In the years when I am dead.

Bliss Carman – A Concise Bibliography

Poetry Collections
Low Tide on Grand Pre: A Book of Lyrics (1893)
Songs from Vagabondia (1894)
A Seamark: A Threnody for Robert Louis Stevenson (1895)
Behind the Arras: A Book of the Unseen (1895)
More Songs from Vagabondia (1896)
Ballads of Lost Haven: A Book of the Sea (1897)
By the Aurelian Wall: And Other Elegies (1898)
A Winter Holiday (1899)
Last Songs from Vagabondia (1901)
Ballads and Lyrics (1902)
Ode on the Coronation of King Edward (1902)
Pipes of Pan: From the Book of Myths (1902)
Pipes of Pan: From the Green Book of the Bards (1903)
Pipes of Pan: Songs of the Sea Children (1904)
Pipes of Pan: Songs from a Northern Garden (1904)
Pipes of Pan: From the Book of Valentines (1905)
Sappho: One Hundred Lyrics (1904)
Poems (1905)
The Rough Rider: And Other Poems (1909)
A Painter's Holiday, and Other Poems (1911)
Echoes from Vagabondia (1912)
April Airs: A Book of New England Lyrics (1916)
The Man of The Marne: And Other Poems (1918)
The Vengeance of Noel Brassard: A Tale of the Acadian Expulsion (1919)
Far Horizons (1925)
Later Poems (1926)
Sanctuary: Sunshine House Sonnets (1929)
Wild Garden (1929)
Bliss Carman's Poems (1931)

Drama
Bliss Carman & Mary Perry King. Daughters of Dawn: A Lyrical Pageant of a Series of Historical Scenes for Presentation with Music and Dancing (1913)
Bliss Carman & Mary Perry King. Earth Deities: And Other Rhythmic Masques (1914)

Prose Collections
The Kinship of Nature (1904)
The Poetry of Life (1905)
The Friendship of Art (1908)
The Making of Personality (1908)
Talks on Poetry and Life; Being a Series of Five Lectures Delivered Before the University of Toronto, December 1925 (Speech). transcribed by Blanche Hume. 1926.
Bliss Carman's Scrap-Book: A Table of Contents (Pierce, Lorne, editor) (1931)

Editor
The World's Best Poetry (10 volumes) (1904)
The Oxford Book of American Verse (U.S. editor) (1927)
Carman, Bliss; Pierce, Lorne, editors (1935). Our Canadian Literature: Representative Verse, English and French.

www.ingramcontent.com/pod-product-compliance
Lightning Source LLC
Chambersburg PA
CBHW070108070426
42448CB00038B/2328